STAGECOACHES AND THE PONY EXPRESS

SALLY SENZELL ISAACS

Heinemann Library
Chicago, Illinois

© 2004 Heinemann Library
a division of Reed Elsevier Inc.
Chicago, Illinois

Customer Service 888-454-2279

Visit our website at www.heinemannlibrary.com

Produced for Heinemann Library by
    Bender Richardson White.
Editor: Lionel Bender
Designer and Page Makeup: Ben White
Picture Researcher: Cathy Stastny
Production Controller: Kim Richardson

07 06 05 04 03
10 9 8 7 6 5 4 3 2 1

Printed in China, by WKT Company Limited.

Library of Congress Cataloging-in-Publication Data.
Isaacs, Sally Senzell, 1950-
    Stagecoaches and the Pony Express / Sally Senzell Isaacs.
        p. cm. – (The American adventure)
    Summary: An account of the most widely-used delivery
systems in the nineteenth-century United States,
stagecoaches and the Pony Express, discussing their
development and challenges faced during their growth.
    ISBN 1-4034-2508-6 (Library binding
    ISBN 1-4034-4793-4 (Pbk.)
    1. Transportation–United States–History–19th century—
Juvenile literature. 2. Stagecoaches–United States–Juvenile
literature. 3. Pony express–United States–Juvenile literature.
4. Overland Mail Company–Juvenile literature. 5. Postal
service—United States–History–Juvenile literature. [1.
Transportation–History–19th century. 2. Stagecoach lines-
History. 3. Pony express. 4. Overland Mail Company. 5.
Postal service–History. 6. West (U.S.)–History–19th century.]
    I. Title. II. Series: American adventure series
    HE203.I8 2004
    388.3'41'0973–dc22
                                    2003013025

Special thanks to Mike Carpenter and Geof Knight at Heinemann
Library for editorial and design guidance and direction.

Acknowledgments
The producers and publishers are grateful to the following for
permission to reproduce copyright material:
Peter Newark's American Pictures, pages 6, 8, 11, 13, 14, 17,
19, 20, 23, 25, 26.

Illustrations by John James
Maps by Stefan Chabluk
Cover art by John James

Every effort has been made to contact copyright holders of any
material reproduced in this book. Omissions will be rectified in
subsequent printings if notice is given to the publisher.

QUOTATIONS

Major quotations used in this book come from the
following sources. Some of the quotations have
been abridged for clarity.

Page 11: David Campbell quote: From *Pioneer of
1846 Sketch of Hardships Endured by Those Who
Crossed the Plains in '46* written for *The Review* by
David Campbell of Porterville, California and
reprinted in the August 11, 12, and 13th issues of
the *Porterville Recorder* in 1910, from which this
was copied.

Page14: Libeus Barney quote: First published in
the *Bennington (Vermont) Banner* and reprinted in
the Western History Department of the Denver
Public Library.

Page 19: Elijah Wilson quote: From *The Pony
Express Goes Through: An American Saga Told by
Its Heroes* by Howard R. Driggs. New York: J.B.
Lippincott, 1935, page 76.

The Author

Sally Senzell Isaacs is a professional writer and
editor of nonfiction books for children. She
graduated from Indiana University, earning a B.S.
degree in education with majors in American
history and sociology. She is the author of the nine
titles in the *America in the Time of...* series
published by Heinemann Library and of the first
sixteen titles in Heinemann Library's *Picture the
Past* series. Sally Senzell Isaacs lives in New
Jersey with her husband and two children.

The Consultant

Our thanks to Dr. Robert J. Chandler, Senior
Research Historian, Wells Fargo Bank, for his
assistance in the preparation of this book.

Wells Fargo

The name *Wells Fargo* and any representation of a
stagecoach with "Wells Fargo" or variations on it is
a corporate symbol and a registered trademark.

★★★★ ABOUT THIS BOOK

This book is about stagecoaches and the Pony Express in the American West. The term *America* means the United States of America (also called the U.S.) The term *West* refers to land west of the Rocky Mountains. *East* is land east of the Mississippi River. The land in between is referred to as the *Midwest* and the *Great Plains.* Most of the events of the book took place between 1820 and 1900.

Stagecoaches, pulled by four to six horses, were used between eastern cities from the 1700s. They carried passengers and mail. Stagecoach service started in the West much later than it started in the East. The Pony Express was a relay of horse riders that carried mail and news from the East to the West. Stagecoaches and the Pony Express were part of everyday life in the U.S. But by 1900 they had disappeared.

★★★★ CONTENTS

ABOUT THE SERIES

The American Adventure is a series of books about important events that shaped the United States of America. Each book focuses on one event. While learning about the event, the reader will also learn how the people and places of the time influenced the nation's future. The little illustrations at the top left of each two-page article are a symbol of the times. They are identified in the Contents on page 3.

▼ This map shows the United States today, with the borders and names of all the states. Refer to this map, or to the one on pages 28 and 29, to locate places talked about in this book.

AMERICA'S STORY

Throughout the book, the yellow panels, showing a Pony Express saddle, contain information that tells the more general history of the United States of America.

THE FEATURE STORY

The green panels, showing a stagecoach, contain information that tells the specific story of stagecoaches and the Pony Express, this book's feature subjects.

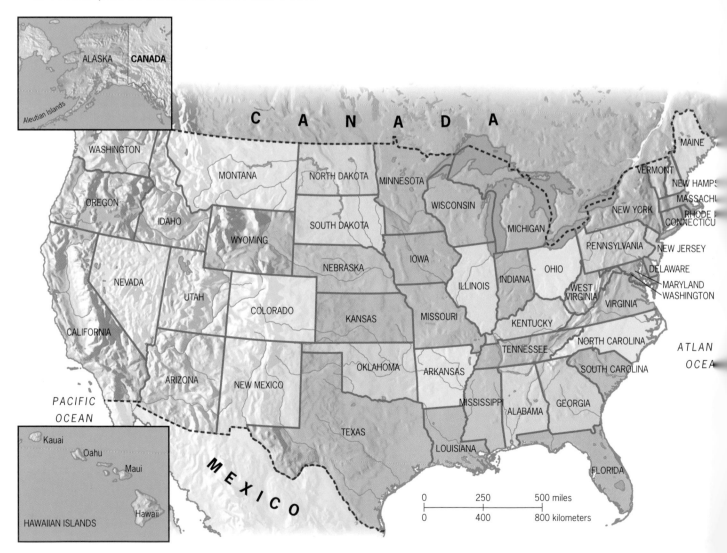

STAGECOACHES AND THE PONY EXPRESS: INTRODUCTION

Transportation has been key to the growth of the United States. The nation started as just a few towns by the Atlantic Ocean. By 1800 its 16 states reached as far west as Kentucky and Tennessee. With the Louisiana Purchase in 1803, the nation doubled in size and reached the Rocky Mountains. By 1853 it stretched to the Pacific Ocean and included all the land that now has the 48 mainland states.

As the nation grew, U.S. citizens moved west. Starting in the 1840s, thousands joined wagon trains from the Missouri River to Oregon and California. They followed trails that were once footpaths of the American Indians and then of explorers, fur traders, and pioneers. Gradually the trails grew into roads. As the population spread across the country, the need arose to send people, goods, and messages farther and faster. Stagecoaches, already traveling between eastern cities, became a popular way to travel in the West. They traveled at about five miles (eight kilometers) an hour and were twice as fast as a horse-drawn wagon or a person on foot. A horse-drawn coach covered long distances by breaking the trip into short sections, each with a stopover point or stage. By 1860 stagecoaches traveled from Missouri and Tennessee to California in about 25 days.

For some people, even stagecoaches were not fast enough to get mail and news out to California. Along came the Pony Express in 1860. This relay of horse riders carried the mail from Missouri to California in ten days. It was an experiment that lasted just eighteen months.

Eventually telegraph wires and railroad tracks crossed the continent. The speed of the telegraph and the amount of mail that trains could carry put the Pony Express out of business. It was just a matter of years before stagecoaches, too, lost their customers—first to the railroads and later to automobiles.

BY RIVERS AND ROADS

Long ago, American Indians paddled carved-out tree trunks across rivers to trade things with one another. Ever since that time, rivers have been important highways for moving goods and people. Until the 1800s, boats moved only as fast as humans could paddle or as the wind could blow.

Then came the steamboats. In 1807 Robert Fulton steered the *Clermont* up the Hudson River from New York City to Albany. Steam hissed out of the engine. Black smoke drifted from the tall smokestack. It seemed, at last, that boats could travel the rivers in any direction, regardless of the wind or currents.

Soon steamboats became a popular and essential way to move from place to place. Between 1812 and 1820 thousands of U.S. citizens left east coast towns to build farms in Indiana, Kentucky, and Ohio. The new farmers needed tools and other goods from eastern towns. They also needed a way to send their crops to markets. Before steamboats, farmers sent their grain, crops, and other goods down the rivers on flat barges. The boats could only float one way with the current. At the destination, people broke up the barges, sold the wood, and walked back home.

STEAMBOAT FACTS
- In 1833 a cabin ticket from St. Louis to Pittsburgh cost $24, while a deck seat cost $8 (these would equal about $480 and $160 at today's prices.)
- In 1844 the *J. M. White* set a speed record by traveling from St. Louis to New Orleans in about a week. The record stood for 25 years.
- The first steamboats burned wood to make steam. Sparks from the burning wood often started fires that destroyed the boats.

▼ If towns were not near a river, stagecoaches like this one carried passengers and freight. This coach carried mail in 1795.

New towns

By 1820 Fulton and his partners were sending steamboats on the Ohio, Mississippi, and Missouri Rivers. Towns grew up by the rivers. Restaurants, stores, and banks opened to serve the people coming and going from the boat docks. Louisville in Kentucky and Cincinnati in Ohio grew by the Ohio River. St. Louis, Missouri, grew by the Mississippi River. Steamboats brought more business for cotton growers in towns along the Mississippi River in Tennessee, Louisiana, and Mississippi. The boats picked up thousands of bales of cotton and took them to New Orleans to be shipped to the east coast and to Europe.

CANALS
Water travel was difficult between two cities that were not near the same body of water. From 1820 to 1840, workers dug canals between waterways. New York built the Erie Canal to connect Lake Erie to the Hudson River. Pennsylvania built a canal between Pittsburgh and Philadelphia. Ohio, Michigan, Indiana, and Wisconsin also built canals. Canal boats were often pulled by horses or mules that walked on a road beside the canal.

▼ As these men use oars to direct their flatboat, they watch a new steamboat move down the Mississippi River. Steamboats carried passengers and freight. Some steamboat passengers sat inside in comfortable cabins. They paid more for their tickets than passengers who sat outside on the deck next to the barrels, farm machines, and animals.

▼ Floating boats traveled about 2 to 4 miles (3.2 to 6.4 kilometers) per hour. Early steamboats traveled about 12 miles (19.2 kilometers) per hour downstream and about 7 miles (11.2 kilometers) per hour upstream.

MOVING FARTHER WEST

By 1840 U.S. citizens had spread out through the 26 states east of the Missouri River. Explorers traveled beyond the river. Many of them went all the way to Oregon Country. When they returned, they told stories of the great farmland and sunny weather.

In the 1840s thousands of emigrants decided to move west to Oregon. Steamboats could not take these pioneers across the continent. Beyond the Missouri River, people walked and used animal power as their main sources of transportation.

Every spring, families from the East traveled by water to the banks of the Missouri River. In growing towns, such as Independence and St. Joseph, Missouri, they bought mules and oxen, built wagons, and stocked up for a 2,000-mile (3,200-kilometer) walk. The trip to Oregon usually took six months. Four to six animals pulled one wagon loaded with the family's possessions. Sometimes a sick person or grandparent sat in the wagon. A few people rode horses. Everyone else walked. They followed the Oregon Trail across plains, rivers, and mountains. The trail mostly ran beside the Platte, Snake, and Columbia Rivers, along a route mapped out by explorers and fur traders.

The emigrants found the trail both boring and dangerous. Thunderstorms swept across the plains. Early blizzards trapped travelers in the mountains. Sometimes people had to coax their animals across muddy rivers. When the river was deep, the emigrants paid American Indians to take the wagons, animals, and people across on flat rafts. In the steep Blue Mountains of Oregon, the emigrants used ropes to lower the wagons over cliffs.

▶ This is Independence, Missouri, in the 1850s. Emigrants covered regular farm wagons with cotton canvas to protect their belongings from sun, dust, and rain.

8

WAGON TRAINS

For safety and companionship, emigrants traveled together in wagon trains. One of the first wagon trains left Independence, Missouri, on May 22, 1843. There were 200 families including 1,000 men, women, and children. They often walked eleven hours a day. It is estimated that between 300,000 and 500,000 people traveled west on the Oregon Trail between 1810 and 1870.

MOVING WEST

These events sent people westward in the 1840s:

1845 Texas joins the United States.

1847 Thousands of Mormons walk to Utah and settle by the Salt Lake.

1848 From Mexico, the United States gains California, Nevada, Utah, and parts of Wyoming, New Mexico, Colorado, and Arizona.

1848 Gold is found near Sacramento, California.

◀ Boats brought people and freight to the banks of the Ohio, Mississippi, and Missouri Rivers. Wagons pulled by horses, mules, and oxen traveled to towns away from the river. Some of the freight included salted pork from Cincinnati; lumber from the forests of Michigan; coal, nails, and iron from Pittsburgh; and cotton from southern states.

◀ The Oregon Trail from Fort Hall headed more sharply northwest. Some travelers took the California Trail to Sacramento. Mormons traveled the Mormon Trail to the Great Salt Lake in Utah. Traders used the Santa Fe Trail from Missouri to present-day New Mexico.

9

THE SANTA FE TRAIL

In 1821 William Becknell took a wagonload of cloth, needles, and other trinkets from Franklin, Missouri, to Santa Fe, New Mexico, which was part of Mexico. The Mexican citizens, eager to make different clothing, were happy to pay two dollars for cloth that cost just six cents in Missouri.

Becknell repeated this profitable trip many times. The trail he traveled became known as the Santa Fe Trail. It was not a new trail. American Indians and Spanish explorers had used it for hundreds of years. Becknell's wagons were the first wheeled vehicles to travel west of the Missouri River. For the next 60 years, many settlers, traders, and travelers came from the East to Santa Fe. They traded the goods for silver, wool, and mules. A wagon, pulled by oxen, made the trip in six to eight weeks.

FORCED OUT

In 1830 Congress passed the Indian Removal Act, forcing American Indians to move west of the Mississippi River. In 1838, U.S. soldiers rounded up about 13,000 Cherokees and forced them to walk 900 miles (1,440 kilometers) from Georgia to Indian Territory in present-day Oklahoma. About 4,000 Cherokees died in a journey that became known as the Trail of Tears.

10

RAILROAD GROWTH
While horses pulled wagons in the West, railroads grew in the East.
1825 John Stevens experiments with the first steam locomotive in the United States.
1830 The nation has 23 miles (36.8 kilometers) of railroad tracks.
1850 The nation has 9,000 miles (14,400 kilometers) of track.
1854 The first train from the East reaches the Mississippi River.
1856 Sacramento Valley Railroad begins, running a total of 21 miles (33.6-kilometers).

Crossing American Indian land

Becknell's wheels were just the first of thousands to roll over the hunting grounds of American Indians. Many tribes lived on the Great Plains in the middle of the nation. Tribes such as the Comanche, Kiowa, Cheyenne, and Arapaho roamed freely and survived by hunting buffalo. At times, they helped travelers by leading them through difficult parts of the trails. They also sold food and supplies that the travelers needed.

Over the years, the American Indians realized they were losing their land and their way of life. The plains were no longer a peaceful place for them. Wagon trains scared away the buffalo. Settlers wanted to build homes. Railroad companies wanted to build tracks. To defend their land, some American Indians attacked travelers and stole their animals. In return, travelers and soldiers fired guns and cannons at the Indians. Eventually the U.S. government forced the Indians to leave the Great Plains.

▼ In the Southwest, where trees were scarce, Indians built their homes with stone, sand, and mud. Traders usually traveled in groups along the Santa Fe Trail. They were afraid of attacks by American Indian tribes. The Indians had fears of their own. The traffic destroyed their hunting grounds.

▲ This painting is by Robert Lindneux. It shows a wagon train under attack by American Indians. David Campbell wrote about his wagon train in 1846: "Three of our men were killed by the Indians. They used poisoned arrows, and when shot by one of them, the poison would go all through one's system."

GOLD RUSH AND GROWTH

In January 1848 James Marshall was working at John Sutter's sawmill 40 miles (64 kilometers) from Sacramento, California. He noticed something sparkling on the ground. It was gold! From all over the world, all kinds of people dropped everything and rushed to California.

WELLS FARGO TIMELINE
• In 1852 Henry Wells and William Fargo started their company in California. They lived in New York.
• From 1852 to today, the company has offered banking services.
• From 1852 to 1918, it offered a delivery service.
• From 1866 to 1869, the company ran stagecoaches across the country. Before and after those years, its coaches connected to other services, such as steamships, railroads, stagecoaches, and the Pony Express.

More than 85,000 people moved to California between 1848 and 1850. Thousands arrived in wagons that followed the Oregon and California Trails. Thousands more arrived by boat from the East, Europe, and Asia. Everyone quickly bought some tools and headed for the gold mines. Those who got there early had the best chance of getting rich but most miners were disappointed. The most successful people were those who opened businesses. Miners were in constant need of food, clothes, supplies, and entertainment.

Sacramento grew into a bustling town because it was the last stop on the wagon trails before the mines. Its businesses included hotels, blacksmiths, printing shops, bakeries, barber shops, bowling alleys, and hospitals. San Francisco grew into a busy city. Ships docked there, and miners sometimes stayed a few days before heading to the mines. Miners also returned there to spend their gold.

Wells Fargo

Henry Wells and William G. Fargo were two New York businesspeople who started a successful business in San Francisco. In 1852 they opened their first bank and transportation service. At the bank, miners exchanged their gold for money. The Wells Fargo Express service delivered the miners' money, in coins and bills, back to their families in the East. The stagecoaches also carried mail, newspapers, and packages from San Francisco to New York and towns in between. Wells, Fargo and Company opened hundreds of offices throughout the West. It quickly became the West's largest stagecoach business.

▶ People said that Wells Fargo service was faster and safer than other services. Armed guards protected $25,000 worth of gold (valued at about $500,000 today) on this wagon from Great Homestake Mine in Deadwood, South Dakota.

▼ A stagecoach is being unpacked after its arrival. Gold coins and paper bills have been delivered to the Wells Fargo office so that miners may exchange gold dust for real money. Letters from the East will be delivered to the post office, where miners will collect them.

THE FIRST STAGECOACHES

In the East, people and mail had been traveling by stagecoach since the early days of the nation (1780s). Horses pulled the box-shaped vehicle from town to town. Each stop was called a stage. At each stage, the driver picked up mail and passengers, and sometimes changed horses. A trip from Philadelphia to Washington took two days and cost $8 (worth $158 today). Passengers slept overnight at an inn.

PROGRESS ON WHEELS

The gold rush brought thousands of people to California. For the next 20 years, gold and silver were discovered in Colorado, Montana, Arizona, South Dakota, and Nevada. A steady stream of miners and merchants came west. With them came stagecoaches and freight wagons.

Several stagecoach and freight companies began running a service between the Missouri River and towns in the West and Southwest. They carried passengers as well as mail, newspapers, groceries, clothing, machinery, and other items. In 1859, the Pikes Peak Express Company began its stagecoach service from the town of Leavenworth, Kansas, to Denver, Colorado. The trip took about two weeks, and the fare was $125 (worth about $2,600 today), which included some meals and a few places to sleep. In the early days, passengers slept in tents. Later, stagecoach companies built log or sod stations. A married couple lived in each station, took care of the building and animals, and cooked for the passengers and workers.

▲ The U.S. government postal service handled mail throughout the nation. But its service to and around the West was very slow. Wells, Fargo and Company promised faster service and charged two to three times the price. People dropped letters in mailboxes like this one.

One man's ride
In 1859 Libeus Barney rode in a stagecoach to Denver to dig for gold. Here are portions of letters he wrote:
"*April 23* Last night was too cold to rest comfortably. Snow ankle deep and atmosphere cold as zero."
"*May 1* Last night the rain poured in torrents the livelong night, and the wind upset our coach and spilled us out ....
Our mules gave out yesterday, and we were compelled to walk the last 12 miles [19.2 kilometers] to the station."

Dangers
During the summer, the Great Plains were hot and dusty. If passengers were lucky enough to pass a stream, they got out and filled their canteens with water. Then coaches and wagons had to pass through the Rocky Mountains. With a heavy coach or wagon behind them, the animals sometimes slipped and overturned. When this happened, the people walked down the mountain to the next station.

▼ Bandits have their eye on a trailer behind a wagon, which is carrying gold from the mine to a bank. They hope to steal a fortune and not dig for it. Other wagons are taking groceries, clothing, mining equipment, dynamite, and other supplies to the gold mines. Mining companies have blasted out the side of this mountain to try to get to the gold below the surface.

BIG BUSINESS

In the 1850s the U.S. government hired the freight company of Russell, Major, and Waddell to transport thousands of tons of supplies from Kansas to the West and Southwest. The company had more than 750 employees, including drivers, blacksmiths, and freight handlers. Between 1858 and 1859, the freight company sent 4,000 wagons and 40,000 oxen for their deliveries to mines, ranches, and soldiers at government forts.

SHARING A RIDE

For a three-week trip, nine people were squeezed together in a full-size stagecoach. Each person had only about 15 inches (38 centimeters) of seat space. Each person was allowed 25 pounds (11.4 kilograms) of baggage. Most nights, passengers slept sitting up in their seats. During the day they passed the time reading or talking. Passengers brought some food. When the coach stopped at a station, the meal was often bread, pork, coffee, and beans.

OVERLAND MAIL COMPANY

In 1850 California became the 31st state in the nation. Nearly 92,600 people lived there. Almost immediately, those people demanded that the U.S. government give them faster mail service.

CIVIL WAR EFFECTS
The Overland Mail Company changed its route in 1861. That year, southern states left the nation, and the Civil War began. The U.S. government took the mail route out of the South. It traveled the Central Route through Denver and Salt Lake City to San Francisco. The war ended in 1865.

Members of Congress agreed to pay a stagecoach company to take the mail from Mississippi River towns to California. In 1857 they gave the contract to the Overland Mail Company, headed by John Butterfield. Congress chose the route, starting at railroad stations in Memphis, Tennessee, and St. Louis, Missouri. These two routes joined in Fort Smith, Arkansas, and followed the Ox-Bow Route (named because of its U-shape) across Texas, New Mexico, Arizona, and southern California to San Francisco. According to the contract, Butterfield's coaches had to make the 2,795-mile (4,472-kilometer) trip in 25 days or less. Passengers rode on the stagecoaches, too.

Much of the route crossed American Indian land. Choctaw and Chickasaw farmers and ranchers lived in Texas. Butterfield paid them to set up stage stations on their land. In Arizona, the trail crossed Apache land. The Apache were known for attacking intruders. Butterfield tried to hire drivers and station masters who were friendly with the Indians.

Butterfield's Rules
The Overland Company was a successful business, with 1,500 animals and 500 wagons and coaches. Butterfield had strict rules for his employees. *Rules for the station masters:* Meals must be served on time. Have well-rested animals ready for the next stagecoach; you'll hear a trumpet blast when the stagecoach is 2 miles (3.2 kilometers) away. If a driver becomes sick or hurt, the station master must take over the drive. *Rules for drivers:* Keep the passengers and mail safe. Keep to the schedule.

CHARLEY'S SECRET

One of the most famous stagecoach drivers was Charley Parkhurst. People told many tales about this tough and talented westerner. Charley stopped a holdup by a bandit by filling his backside with bullets! Charley took a team of horses around a sharp bend on a cliff without touching the edge!

What most people did not know was that Charley was a woman who disguised herself as a man.

▶ A stagecoach of the California-Oregon Stagecoach Company passes Mount Shasta, California, in 1871. Some coaches carried fourteen passengers. Baggage was strapped to the top of the coach. In 1858 the trip from Memphis or St. Louis to California cost $200 (worth over $4,000 today). Shorter trips cost 10 cents a mile (1.6 kilometers).

▼ Bandits wave their guns and make the driver hand over the box of gold. Bandits also stole money from passengers. Usually an armed guard, called the shotgun messenger, sat next to the driver to protect everyone.

THE PONY EXPRESS

The stagecoaches of John Butterfield's Overland Mail Company delivered mail twice a week. They could carry letters and newspapers from St. Louis to San Francisco in about 18 to 24 days. But in 1860, Californians wanted their mail and news faster.

In 1860 William Russell, of the freight company Russell, Majors, and Waddell, announced his plans for the Pony Express. The company promised twice-a-week delivery from St. Joseph, Missouri, to San Francisco, California, in ten days. Perhaps Russell learned about the horse relay systems used in ancient Rome and China. He probably knew about Ben Franklin's relay mail service in the 1750s. In Russell's plan, a relay team of riders moved a saddlebag full of mail across the country. One rider passed the saddlebag to another about every 75 miles (120 kilometers).

Pony Express riders

It took brave, young men to ride for the Pony Express. Each rider raced for about ten miles (sixteen kilometers) to a relay station. There he threw his saddlebag, called a *mochila,* over a new horse and galloped off again. After about eight hours, the rider stopped at a home station. A new rider took over while the first rider waited for a delivery in the opposite direction. The route went through eight states across icy rivers and streams, over the Rocky Mountains and Sierra Nevada, and through deserts. It ended in Sacramento, where the mail was loaded on a riverboat to San Francisco.

A short career

The Pony Express started on April 3, 1860. It delivered about 35,000 letters and covered 616,000 miles (985,600 kilometers). It provided the fastest communication service in the country. But in the end it lost money. The company had high expenses, with its stations, horses, and workers. Then, in the summer of 1860, there was the Paiute War. The Paiute Indians in Nevada and Utah revolted after hundreds of miners and settlers invaded their hunting grounds and cut down trees. The Paiute brought a stop to the Pony Express for four weeks. In October 1861 the service became unnecessary when the nation's transcontinental telegraph system was completed. The Pony Express ended shortly afterward.

▼ Being a Pony Express rider was not a job for the fearful. Here, a rider dashes through an American Indian burial ground and is being chased by Indians. The Paiute were the main tribe that staged a campaign against the Pony Express. During the Paiute War, they destroyed seven stations and killed 150 horses and 16 employees. The Pony Express had to rebuild afterward.

BUFFALO BILL
"Buffalo Bill" Cody was one of the most famous Pony Express riders. He was just fifteen when he got the job. There are hundreds of stories about Bill's bravery. One says that Bill rode into a station to find that bandits had killed the next rider. Bill took the mail another 76 miles (121.5 kilometers) and then made a return trip. He rode a record-setting 384 miles (614.5 kilometers) without a long break.

PONY EXPRESS PRICES
The Pony Express had high expenses—more than $25,000 a month. In April 1860, the cost to mail a letter was $5 per half-ounce (16 grams). To cover the expenses, the company needed to carry 5,000 letters a month at $5 a letter. The average number of letters was just 1,944. As a result, the company lost at least $15,280 a month, (worth about $305,000 today.)

▲ This letter includes the Wells Fargo and the Pony Express "postage stamps." Wells Fargo ran a Pony Express service between Virginia City, Nevada Territory, and San Francisco from 1862 to 1865.

19

THE TELEGRAPH

Stagecoaches did their best to deliver mail to the West within a few weeks. The Pony Express and railroads did it in about ten days. But some messages seemed too important to wait at all. In 1860 Congress decided to help pay for a transcontinental telegraph system.

The telegraph system was invented by Samuel Morse in 1837. The telegraph is a machine that uses electricity to send a code of dots and dashes. The dots and dashes represent letters of the alphabet. The code is sent over wires that are strung between poles. In 1843, the U.S. government gave $30,000 (worth about $750,000 today) to Morse to build a telegraph line between Washington, D.C., and Baltimore, Maryland. By 1851, the United States had more than 50 telegraph companies scattered over the country. That year, railroads started using the telegraph. They sent messages to tell engineers when other trains were late or stalled on the tracks.

Wires across the continent

In 1861 Congress paid a company called Western Union Telegraph Company to complete a transcontinental telegraph system. The company connected new lines to existing ones until a telegraph system stretched from coast to coast. It was possible for the entire nation to receive news, such as election results, business news, and weather reports, within seconds. From 1861 to 1865, soldiers from the northern states and southern states fought the Civil War. Newspaper reporters near the war wrote stories and telegraphed them across the nation. Some families sent news of births and deaths by telegraph.

TELEPHONES

On February 14, 1876, Elisha Gray and Alexander Graham Bell independently filed for patents on telephones that let people talk to each other from different places. Bell filed two hours earlier and got the patent. From 1877 to 1879, Western Union Company was in the telephone business. Then Bell's company sued Western Union and made them stop.

▶ Pony Express stations were turned into stagecoach and railroad stations. Here, a telegraph agent works inside a train station. People came to the station to send their telegraph messages. If important news came over the telegraph wires, this woman would be the first to know it. Trains and stagecoaches still carried thousands of pieces of mail.

▼ Telegraph poles sprang up like weeds. Soon 23,000 miles (36,800 kilometers) of wire crisscrossed the nation. Many lines followed railroad routes. Sometimes a Pony Express rider galloped by and told the telegraph crew about fellow workers down the line.

MAIL TIMELINE
1639 First post office in U.S. opens in a tavern in Boston.
1836 Trains start to carry mail.
1847 First postage stamps are used.
Early 1860s Mail carriers start to deliver to homes.
1918 Planes carry mail for people who pay more for airmail service.
1963 Computers sort mail by ZIP codes.

Progress

The transcontinental telegraph system was completed on October 24, 1861. Two days later, the Pony Express closed down. By 1866 a telegraph cable extended under the Atlantic Ocean, and telegraph service began between the United States and Europe. U.S. citizens depended on the telegraph system until the 1890s. Then, just as the telegraph replaced the Pony Express, the telephone replaced the telegraph.

TO THE PACIFIC COAST

By the 1860s U.S. citizens lived all across the continent. Some moved to ranches in Texas. Some moved to Nebraska farms. Thousands of immigrants moved to the United States from other countries. Some worked in eastern factories that sent furniture and other goods west. Others moved to the West.

More people than ever traveled all the way to the Pacific Coast. A trip from Atchison, Kansas, to San Francisco took about three weeks. People took a train or steamboat to the Missouri River. Then they rode a stagecoach to central California. A train took them to Sacramento, where they caught a steamboat to San Francisco. The cost was $250 to $500. In today's money, that was eighteen times the cost of an ordinary plane ticket from Missouri to California.

To go from New York to California, many people traveled by ship. It took three to six months to sail around South America. A quicker route took one month. Ships from New York docked at Panama. After 1855 people crossed Panama by train. Then they boarded other ships taking them north to California.

TRANSCONTINENTAL RAILROAD TIMELINE
July 1862 President Lincoln signs the Pacific Railroad Act to help pay for the railroad.
January 1863 Central Pacific lays its first rails.
December 1863 Union Pacific starts work, but few tracks are laid until the Civil War ends in 1865.
May 1869 Union Pacific and Central Pacific tracks meet at Promontory, Utah.

By 1869 the United States had a transcontinental railroad. The Central Pacific Railroad built tracks from Sacramento eastward. The Union Pacific built westward from Omaha, Nebraska. The tracks met at Promontory, Utah. Tracks from all directions connected to these tracks. Thanks to the railroad, people could travel from New York to California in ten days.

▶ A stagecoach pulls up to a station in Utah. The horses will get food and water. Passengers might buy a meal for about a dollar. The men in front are measuring the land because railroad tracks will soon be built here. Telegraph wires already connect this town with many others.

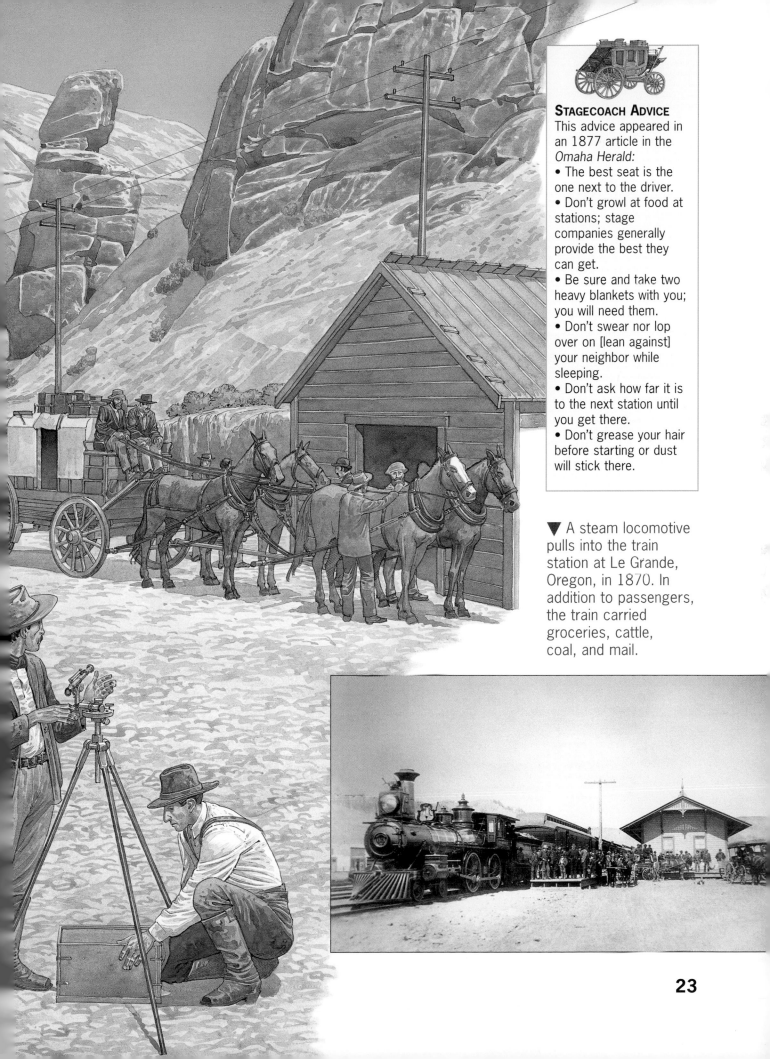

▼ A steam locomotive pulls into the train station at Le Grande, Oregon, in 1870. In addition to passengers, the train carried groceries, cattle, coal, and mail.

CONNECTING THE COUNTRY

As railroad tracks crossed the Great Plains, small towns grew in the center of the country. Between 1870 and 1890, the population of Kansas City grew from 3,000 to 37,000. Omaha grew from 16,000 to 140,000.

By 1870 the nation had 52,922 miles (846,752 kilometers) of railroad tracks, enough to circle twice around the world. Another 110,655 miles (177,048 kilometers) were added by 1890. In Texas, towns such as Dallas and San Antonio grew into cities. Texas ranchers loaded thousands of cattle onto trains and sent them east for the booming beef business. Iron, lumber, and food also sped across the country in railroad cars.

Railroad companies set prices for shipping goods across the country. Some people thought the prices were unfair. For example, it cost $1 to send 100 pounds (45.5 kilograms) of cloth from New York to California. It cost $2.30 to send the same shipment from New York to Utah. Railroad companies knew that factories could use ships to send cloth to California so they made their price low. Ships could not reach Utah, so with no competition, they set a higher price. In 1887 Congress began making laws to make transportation rates more fair.

RAILROADS AND AMERICAN INDIANS

Railroads brought more problems to the American Indians. Railroad workers and passengers killed millions of buffalo. Sometimes the meat was used to feed railroad workers, but many times, people shot the animals for sport.

Railroad tracks brought more settlers to the West. Little by little, the U.S. government took land from the American Indians and moved them to reservations away from the settlers. By 1893 almost all American Indians lived on reservations.

▶ The people of this western town receive supplies by train and horse-drawn wagon. The wagon brings goods from a nearby town. The train carries clothing and other items from farther away. Before the railroad was built, people made most of the things they needed. Now the stores are full of factory-made goods from the East.

Comfort and speed

Through the 1880s stagecoaches continued to roll in and out of the nation's towns. They were still important for short journeys and trips to places away from the railroads. But stagecoaches were no competition for passengers who cared about speed and comfort. By 1893 a train set a record by traveling 100 miles (160 kilometers) an hour. Even at slower rates, a coast-to-coast trip could take less than a week. A man named George Pullman designed railroad cars with soft, roomy seats and fancy dining-room tables. His sleeper cars had beds that folded down from the wall and long green curtains for privacy.

▶ Compared to travelers in the fancy Pullman cars, these travelers had less expensive and less comfortable seats.

STAGECOACH MARY

Mary Fields was born a slave in Tennessee in 1832. In her younger days, she worked in a Catholic school and later ran a café. She grew up to be a well-known stagecoach driver in Montana. Fields fit right in with the Wild West days of the late 1800s. She was tough and adventurous. She drove a U.S. mail coach, never missing a day of work until she was almost 80 years old. People called her Stagecoach Mary.

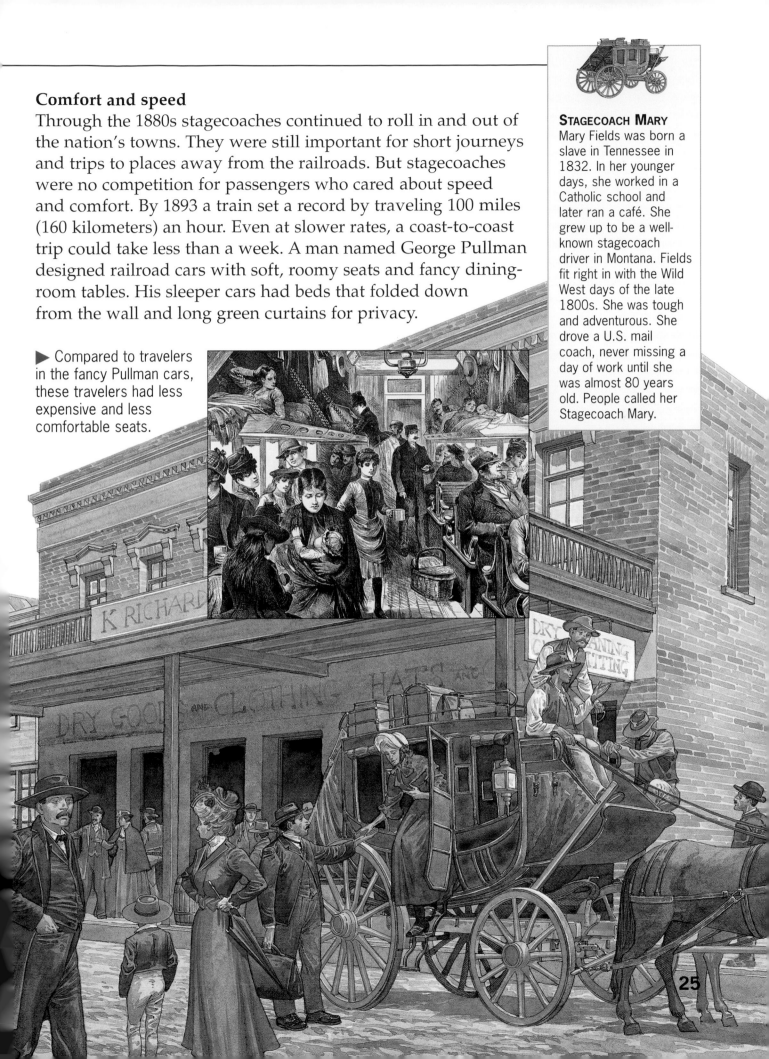

MODERN TRANSPORTATION

Adventurous U.S. citizens had always dreamed of moving to the frontier. The frontier is the name for the wilderness that lies outside the settled area. By 1890 the United States Census Bureau looked at reports that told where U.S. citizens lived. The Bureau announced that the country had no more frontier.

HENRY FORD
In 1900 a car cost more than $1,000. Only rich people bought them. Then Henry Ford started the Ford Motor Company in Michigan. With his assembly-line system, workers built a car every 12 1/2 hours. The price dropped to $825. By 1914 Ford's workers could make a car within 1 1/2 hours. By 1924 the price dropped to $290. (That is worth about $3,000 today.) Ordinary people could buy cars.

In 1889 the U.S. government began offering the last of the wide-open spaces to settlers. On April 22, nearly 100,000 settlers rushed out to grab 3,125 square miles (8,090 square kilometers) of Indian Territory. Town such as Oklahoma City and Guthrie, Oklahoma, appeared overnight. Railroads brought more settlers to the area. Even as trains sped throughout the country, people still used stagecoaches to places between railroad towns.

By the end of the 1800s, stagecoaches were in their final days. The automobile was coming. Before the 1900s inventors in Europe and the United States experimented with a carriage powered by steam or batteries. In the U.S. in 1893, Charles and J. Frank Duryea invented the gasoline-powered car. At first people laughed at the "horseless carriage." Only 8,000 U.S. citizens owned cars in 1900. But by 1917 there were more than 4.5 million cars on the nation's roads.

More incredible ways to move
By the early 1900s, electric elevated trains ran in Chicago, Boston, and New York. They ran on tracks above the traffic. Boston and New York also had underground trains, called subways. To add to the excitement of transportation, in 1903 people worldwide heard the news from the U.S. of the Wright Brothers. Orville and Wilbur Wright built a machine that could fly.

▶ This is Broadway, one of New York City's busiest streets, in 1880. Telephone and telegraph lines crisscross the streets.

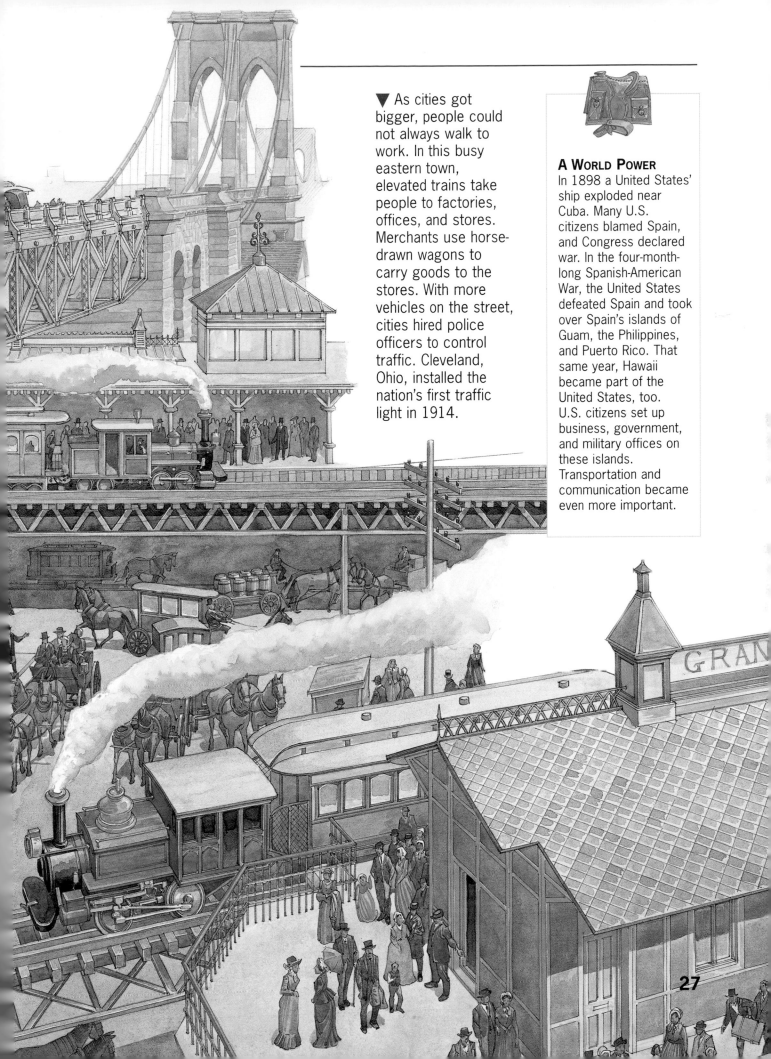

▼ As cities got bigger, people could not always walk to work. In this busy eastern town, elevated trains take people to factories, offices, and stores. Merchants use horse-drawn wagons to carry goods to the stores. With more vehicles on the street, cities hired police officers to control traffic. Cleveland, Ohio, installed the nation's first traffic light in 1914.

A WORLD POWER
In 1898 a United States' ship exploded near Cuba. Many U.S. citizens blamed Spain, and Congress declared war. In the four-month-long Spanish-American War, the United States defeated Spain and took over Spain's islands of Guam, the Philippines, and Puerto Rico. That same year, Hawaii became part of the United States, too. U.S. citizens set up business, government, and military offices on these islands. Transportation and communication became even more important.

27

HISTORICAL MAP OF THE UNITED STATES

This is a map of the United States in 1880. The nation had 38 states. The rest of the mainland territories would become states by 1912. Traffic on the stagecoach trails was greatest from 1850 to 1880. By 1880 the nation had more than 93,000 miles (148,800 kilometers) of railroad tracks, and more under construction. By 1893 five transcontinental railroads crossed the country.

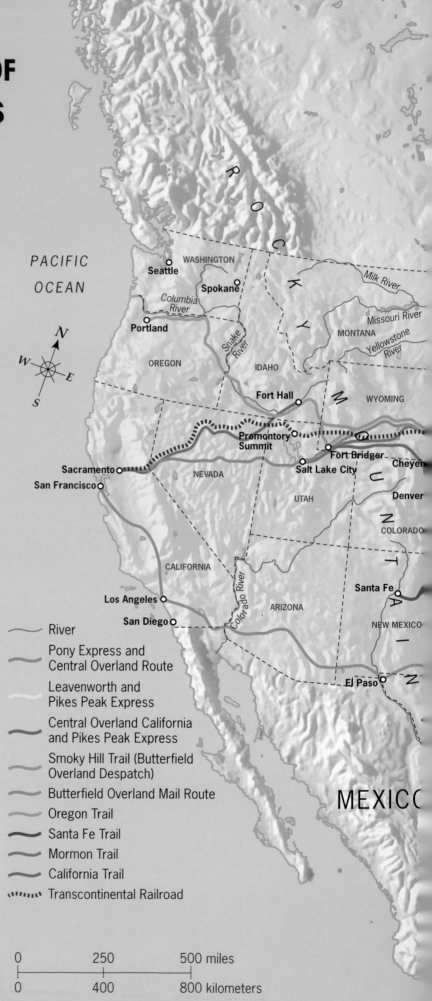

PACIFIC OCEAN

Seattle
WASHINGTON
Spokane
Columbia River
Portland
OREGON
Snake River
IDAHO
Fort Hall
Promontory Summit
Sacramento
NEVADA
San Francisco
UTAH
CALIFORNIA
Colorado River
Los Angeles
San Diego
ARIZONA

MONTANA
Milk River
Missouri River
Yellowstone River
WYOMING
Fort Bridger
Salt Lake City
Cheyen
Denver
COLORADO
Santa Fe
NEW MEXICO
El Paso

MEXICO

ROCKY MOUNTAIN

Legend:
— River
— Pony Express and Central Overland Route
— Leavenworth and Pikes Peak Express
— Central Overland California and Pikes Peak Express
— Smoky Hill Trail (Butterfield Overland Despatch)
— Butterfield Overland Mail Route
— Oregon Trail
— Santa Fe Trail
— Mormon Trail
— California Trail
······ Transcontinental Railroad

Kauai
Oahu
Maui
Hawaii
HAWAIIAN ISLANDS

ALASKA
CANADA
Aleutian Islands

| 0 | 250 | 500 miles |
| 0 | 400 | 800 kilometers |

Hudson Bay

C A N A D A

Lake Superior

Lake Huron

Lake Ontario

NORTH DAKOTA

MINNESOTA

WISCONSIN

Missouri River

SOUTH DAKOTA

Minneapolis

Mississippi River

MICHIGAN

Lake Michigan

Milwaukee

Detroit

Lake Erie

Cleveland

NEBRASKA

Omaha

IOWA

Chicago

Pittsburgh

OHIO

INDIANA

ulesburg

St. Joseph

Atchison

ILLINOIS

Leavenworth

Kansas City

Independence

St. Louis

Ohio River

WEST VIRGINIA

KANSAS

MISSOURI

KENTUCKY

OKLAHOMA

ARKANSAS

Memphis

Mississippi River

TENNESSEE

Fort Smith

Birmingham

Atlanta

MISSISSIPPI

ALABAMA

GEORGIA

LOUISIANA

TEXAS

New Orleans

Houston

San Antonio

Rio Grande River

MAINE

VERMONT

NEW HAMPSHIRE

MASSACHUSETTS

Boston

RHODE ISLAND

NEW YORK

CONNECTICUT

Hudson River

New York City

PENNSYLVANIA

Delaware River

Philadelphia

NEW JERSEY

DELAWARE

MARYLAND

Washington, D.C.

VIRGINIA

James River

APPALACHIAN MOUNTAINS

NORTH CAROLINA

SOUTH CAROLINA

Charleston

Savannah

Jacksonville

FLORIDA

St. Lawrence

ATLANTIC OCEAN

GULF OF MEXICO

29

CARIBBEAN SEA

GLOSSARY

American Indians people in America whose ancestors lived there before European explorers and settlers arrived

armed carrying a weapon such as a gun

bandit robber, usually part of a gang

barge long boat with a flat bottom

canal body of water made by people. A canal connects one body of water to another and is like a water highway.

canvas strong cloth usually made of cotton and mostly used for tents and sails

Civil War (1861 to 1865) in the United States, a war between the North and the South. The slave-holding South wanted independence. The North wanted to keep the country together.

Congress part of the U.S. government in which representatives make laws

crops plants grown to provide food or to sell

emigrant person who leave his or her home to move to a new area or country

freight goods that are carried by wagons, trucks, trains, or ships

gold rush starting in 1849, the time when people rushed to California to find gold

Great Plains enormous area of grassland east of the Rocky Mountains. North to south, it stretches 2,500 miles (4,020 kilometers) from Canada to Texas.

home station comfortable house or other larger building where a Pony Express rider would stop to rest and eat while another rider or stagecoach continued to transport the mail along the route

Indian Territory land mostly in present-day Oklahoma that was set aside by the U.S. government for the American Indians

locomotive engine used to pull a train

Mormon member of the Church of Jesus Christ of Latter-day Saints. Many Mormons moved to present-day Utah in the 1850s to avoid criticism and attacks for their beliefs.

patent legal document that gives only the inventor of an item the rights to make or sell that item

plains wide area of flat or gently rolling land

relay station small building or structure where Pony Express riders changed horses

reservation area of land set aside by the government for American Indians to live

settler person who makes a home in a new place

slave person who is owned by another person and is usually made to work for that person. After 1865, slavery was illegal in the United States.

sod piece of earth with grass and roots

station master person who lived and/or worked at a stagecoach, Pony Express, or railroad station. The person took care of horses and mules and sometimes provided food for the drivers, riders, and passengers.

sue to start a legal case in which a judge will make someone stop an action or pay money as a penalty for a wrongdoing

telegraph machine that sends messages over electric wires in the form of a code

territory in the United States, an area of land that was not yet a state. Once a territory had 60,000 citizens, it could be admitted as a new state.

trader person who purchases things by exchanging one kind of goods for another. Traders traveled from one place to another to exchange things.

transcontinental across a continent

wagon train group of covered wagons that traveled to the West together

TIMELINE OF EVENTS IN THIS BOOK

1807 Steamboats begin carrying passengers and freight in the United States. Robert Fulton's *Clermont* steams up the Hudson River in New York.

1821 William Becknell begins trading in New Mexico by traveling the Santa Fe Trail

1825 Workers complete the Erie Canal that connects the Great Lakes to the Atlantic Ocean

1830 Congress passes the Indian Removal Act to move American Indians to Indian Territory

1843 The first organized wagon trains head for Oregon and California

1845 Texas joins the United States

1846 The United States signs the Oregon Treaty with Britain. Present-day Washington, Oregon, Idaho, and part of Montana and Wyoming become U.S. territories.

1847 Mormons walk to Utah to settle by the Great Salt Lake

1848 Gold is discovered near Sacramento, California, starting the gold rush

1848 War with Mexico ends. California, Nevada, Utah, and parts of Wyoming, New Mexico, Colorado, and Arizona become part of the United States.

1852 Wells, Fargo and Company starts its first bank and express services

1853 In the Gadsden Purchase, the United States buys southern Arizona and New Mexico from Mexico

1858 John Butterfield's Overland Mail Company starts delivering mail between the Midwest and California

1859 Silver is discovered in an area called the Comstock Lode in Nevada

1860 to 1861 The Pony Express delivers mail from Missouri to California

1861 to 1865 Northern and southern states fight the Civil War

1861 Transcontinental telegraph service begins

1862 Congress passes the Homestead Act, giving land to settlers in the West

1864 George Pullman builds the first railroad car designed for sleeping

1866 Telegraph service begins across the Atlantic Ocean

1869 The Union Pacific and Central Pacific Railroads complete the first transcontinental railroad

1876 Alexander Graham Bell gets a patent for his telephone

1889 The first land rush in Oklahoma takes place. The U.S. government allows settlers to claim land that had been formally given to American Indians.

1896 Henry Ford builds his first gasoline-powered car

FURTHER READING

Kroll-Smith, Steve. *Pony Express!* New York: Scholastic, Inc., 2000.

Markel, Rita J. *Your Travel Guide to America's Old West.* Minneapolis, Minn.: Lerner Publishing, 2003.

McCormick, Anita Louise. *The Pony Express in American History.* Berkeley Heights, N.J.: Enslow Publishers, 2001.

Riddle, John. *The Pony Express.* Broomall, Penn.: Mason Crest, 2002.

Staeger, Rob. *The Boom Towns.* Broomall, Penn.: Mason Crest, 2002.

Staff, Celebration Press. *West by Stagecoach.* Boston: Celebration Press, 2002.

William, Jean Kinney. *The Pony Express.* Minneapolis, Minn.: Compass Point Books, 2002.

PLACES TO VISIT

Mahaffie Farmstead and Stagecoach Stop
Historic Site
110 Kansas City Road
Olathe, KS 66051
Telephone: (913) 782–6972

Wells Fargo History Museum
1000 Second Street
Sacramento, CA 95814
Telephone: (916) 440–4263

Wells Fargo History Museum
420 Montgomery Street
San Francisco, CA 94163
Telephone: (415) 396–2619

Wells Fargo History Museum
333 South Grand
Los Angeles, CA 90071
Telephone: (213) 253–7166

Wells Fargo History Museum
Sixth & Marquette
Minneapolis, MN 55479
Telephone: (612) 667–4210

Pony Express Museum
914 Penn Street
St. Joseph, MO 64503
Telephone: (816) 279–5059
or (800) 530–5930

Stagecoach Museum
322 South Main Street
Lusk, WY 82225
Telephone (307) 334–3444

INDEX